The Spirit of 1776

THE SPIRIT OF
1776

Life, Liberty and the Pursuit of Happiness
During the American Revolution

Selected by Peter Seymour

HALLMARK EDITIONS

Illustration Acknowledgments

Cover and Title Page: *The Spirit of '76* by Archibald M. Willard. This painting hangs in the office of the Board of Selectmen in Marblehead, Massachusetts. Page 4: *The Horse America Throwing His Master*. Courtesy the Library of Congress. Pages 16-17: *The Bloody Massacre* by Paul Revere. Courtesy the Metropolitan Museum of Art. Gift of Mrs. Russell Sage, 1910. Page 29: *E. Noyes, Tavern Sign*. Courtesy the Shelburne Museum, Inc., Shelburne, Vermont. Pages 40-41: *The Battle of Princeton* by William Mercer. Courtesy the Historical Society of Pennsylvania, Philadelphia. Pages 52-53: *Celebration of the Fourth of July* by J. L. Krimmel. Courtesy the Historical Society of Pennsylvania, Philadelphia.

Cover and Title Page: *The Spirit of '76* by Archibald M. Willard. This famous painting shows the strength and determination of the colonial cause.

THE SPIRIT OF
1776

The Horse America Throwing His Master. This early cartoon etching depicts the thirteen American colonies in the form of a horse throwing its rider, King George III of England.

'THE TIMES THAT TRY MEN'S SOULS'

The American colonists had left England to escape British oppression. But tyranny did not end, and the Americans again banded together. One of the great influences on public opinion against Great Britain was the writing of Tom Paine. He wrote the booklet "Common Sense" and followed this with a series of stirring pamphlets entitled "The American Crisis," from which the following famous passage is taken:

These are the times that try men's souls. The summer soldier and the sunshine patriot will, in this crisis, shrink from the service of their country; but he that stands it *now* deserves the love and thanks of man and woman. Tyranny, like hell, is not easily conquered; yet we have this consolation with us, that the harder the conflict, the more glorious the triumph. What we obtain too cheap, we esteem too lightly: it is dearness only that gives every thing its value. Heaven knows how to put a proper price upon its goods; and it would be strange indeed if so celestial an article as FREEDOM should not be highly rated. Britain, with an army to enforce her tyranny, has declared that she has a right (*not only to* TAX) but "TO BIND *us in* ALL CASES WHATSOEVER," and if being *bound in that manner* is not slavery, then there is not such a thing as slavery upon earth. Even the expression is impious; for so unlimited a power can belong only to God. ·

THE BOSTON TEA PARTY

Angered at being forced by Britain to accept tea as a monopoly of the East India Company, a group of colonists took it upon themselves to dump the tea before it was put ashore in Boston harbor. Disguised as Indians, the group threw 342 chests of tea overboard. George Hewes, a member of the raiding party, describes the event:

The tea destroyed was contained in three ships, lying near each other, at what was called at that time Griffin's wharf, and [they] were surrounded by armed ships of war; the commanders of which had publicly declared, that if the rebels, as they were pleased to style the Bostonians, should not withdraw their opposition to the landing of the tea before a certain day, the 17th day of December, 1773, they should on that day force it on shore, under the cover of their cannon's mouth. On the day preceding the seventeenth, there was a meeting of the citizens of the county of Suffolk, convened at one of the churches in Boston, for the purpose of consulting on what measures might be considered expedient to prevent the landing of the tea. . . .

[That] evening, I dressed myself in the costume of an Indian, equipped with a small hatchet, which I and my associates denominated the tomahawk, with which, and a club, after having painted my face and hands with coal dust in the shop of a blacksmith, I repaired to Griffin's wharf, where the ships lay that contained the tea. When I first appeared in the street, after being thus disguised, I fell in with many who were dressed, equipped, and painted as I was, and who fell in with me, and marched in order to the place of our destination. . . .

We were immediately ordered to board all the ships at the same time. The commander of the division to which I belonged appointed me boatswain, and ordered me to go to the captain and demand of him the keys to the hatches and a dozen candles. I made the demand accordingly, and the captain promptly replied, and delivered the articles; but requested me at the same time to do no damage to the ship or rigging. We then were ordered by our commander to open the hatches, and take out all the chests of tea and throw them overboard, and we immediately proceeded to execute his orders; first cutting and splitting the chests with our tomahawks, so as thoroughly to expose them to the effects of the water. . . .

The next morning it was discovered that very considerable quantities of tea were floating upon the surface of the water; and to prevent the possibility of its being saved for use, a number of small boats were manned by sailors and citizens, who rowed them into those parts of the harbor wherever the tea was visible, and by beating it with oars and paddles, so thoroughly drenched it, as to render its entire destruction inevitable.

'GIVE ME LIBERTY OR GIVE ME DEATH!'

Patrick Henry's speech to the Virginia Convention, March 23, 1775, was considered close to treason by some . . . perhaps because it so vehemently summed up the spirit underlying the colonists' fight to become an independent nation!

It is in vain, sir, to extenuate the matter. Gentlemen may cry, "Peace! peace!"—but there is no peace. The war is actually begun! The next gale that sweeps from the north will bring to our ears the clash of resounding arms! Our brethren are already in the field! Why stand we here idle? What is it that gentlemen wish? What would they have? Is life so dear, or peace so sweet, as to be purchased at the price of chains and slavery? Forbid it, Almighty God! I know not what course others may take; but as for me, give me liberty or give me death!

PLEDGE AGAINST TEA: 1775

Various women's groups responded to the British tea monopoly by boycotting the use of tea. Here, the society of the Patriotic Ladies in North Carolina issues a pledge:

Farewell the teaboard with your gaudy attire,
Ye cups and saucers that I did admire;
To my cream pot and tongs I now bid adieu;
That pleasure's all fled that I once found in you...
No more shall my teapot so generous be
In filling the cups with this pernicious tea,
For I'll fill it with water and drink out the same
Before I'll lose *Liberty*, that dearest name...
Before she shall part I will die in the cause,
For I'll never be governed by tyranny's laws.

THE SHOT HEARD
ROUND THE WORLD

War began with the battles of Lexington and Concord on April 19, 1775. Emerson's famous poem Concord Hymn *and excerpts from Longfellow's poetic narrative* Paul Revere's Ride *recreate the drama of that historic time:*

From PAUL REVERE'S RIDE

Listen, my children, and you shall hear
Of the midnight ride of Paul Revere,
On the eighteenth of April, in seventy-five;
Hardly a man is now alive
Who remembers that famous day and year.

He said to his friend, "If the British march
By land or sea from the town tonight,
Hang a lantern aloft in the belfry arch
Of the North Church tower as a signal light,—
One, if by land, and two, if by sea;
And I on the opposite shore will be,
Ready to ride and spread the alarm
Through every Middlesex village and farm,
For the country folk to be up and to arm."

Then he said, "Good night!" and with muffled oar
Silently rowed to the Charlestown shore. . . .

*Later, a friend, positioned in the North Church
Tower, spots a "shadowy something far away . . .
like a bridge of boats" and flashes the signal to
Revere who rushes off to warn the colonists:*

So through the night rode Paul Revere;
And so through the night went his cry of alarm
To every Middlesex village and farm,—
A cry of defiance, and not of fear,
A voice in the darkness, a knock at the door,
And a word that shall echo for evermore!
For, borne on the night-wind of the Past,
Through all our history, to the last,
In the hour of darkness and peril and need,
The people will waken and listen to hear
The hurrying hoof-beats of that steed,
And the midnight message of Paul Revere.

HENRY WADSWORTH LONGFELLOW

CONCORD HYMN

By the rude bridge that arched the flood,
Their flag to April's breeze unfurled,
Here once the embattled farmers stood,
And fired the shot heard round the world.

The foe since in silence slept;
Alike the conqueror silent sleeps;
And Time the ruined bridge has swept
Down the dark stream which seaward creeps.

On this green bank, by this soft stream,
We set today a votive stone;
That memory may their deed redeem,
When, like our sires, our sons are gone.

Spirit, that made those spirits dare
To die, and leave their children free,
Bid Time and Nature gentle spare
The shaft we raise to them and thee.

RALPH WALDO EMERSON

Page 12: John Singleton Copley's *Portrait of Paul Revere*. Gift of Joseph W. Revere, William B. Revere and Edward H. R. Revere. Courtesy the Museum of Fine Arts, Boston, Massachusetts. The painting was probably done about 1765 to pay off a debt to Revere.

13

ABIGAIL TO JOHN ADAMS

*When John Adams was elected a representative
from Massachusetts to the Congress, which was in
session in Philadelphia, it required his first pro-
longed separation from Abigail, his wife of 10
years. The Adams had four children and lived out-
side of Boston, in Braintree, from where Abigail
wrote the following letter on August 19, 1774:*

The great distance between us makes the time appear very long to me. It seems already a month
since you left me. The great anxiety I feel for my
country, for you, and for our family renders the
day tedious and the night unpleasant. The rocks
and quicksands appear upon every side.

What course you can or will take is all wrapped
in the bosom of futurity. Uncertainty and expec-
tation leave the mind great scope. Did ever any
kingdom or state regain its liberty, when once it
was invaded, without bloodshed? I cannot think of
it without horror. Yet we are told that all the misfortunes of Sparta were occasioned by their too
great solicitude for present tranquillity, and from
an excessive love of peace, they neglected the
means of making it sure and lasting. They ought
to have reflected, says Polybius, that, "as there is

nothing more desirable or advantageous than peace, when founded in justice and honor, so there is nothing more shameful, and at the same time more pernicious, when attained by bad measures and purchased at the price of liberty."

I want much to hear from you. I long impatiently to have you upon the stage of action. The first of September, or the month of September, perhaps, may be of as much importance to Great Britain as the Ides of March were to Caesar. I wish you every public as well as private blessing, and that wisdom which is profitable both for instruction and edification, to conduct you in this difficult day. The little flock remember papa, and kindly wish to see him; so does your most affectionate.

Overleaf: The Bloody Massacre, an engraving by Paul Revere. This anti-British cartoon illustrates the apparent ruthlessness of British soldiers against a crowd of unarmed Americans. In actuality, a mob of American toughs had attacked the troops, who fired back in self-defense. Five Americans were killed.

et *BOSTON* on March 5ᵗʰ 1770 by a party of the 29ᵗʰ REGᵗ

BUTCHER'S HALL

crav'd Printed & Sold by PAUL REVERE *BOSTON*

Rage from Anguish Wrung, | But know,FATE summons to that awful GoaL
lab'ring for a Tongue | Where JUSTICE strips the Murd'rer of his Soul:
an ought appease | Should venal C—ts the scandal of the Land,
Victims such as these: | Snatch the relentless Villain from her Hand,
ars for each are shed. | Keen Execrations on this Plate inscrib'd,
h embalms the Dead. | Shall reach a JUDGE who never can be brib'd.

MAVERICK, JAMᶺ CALDWELL, CRISPUS ATTUCKS & PATᴷCARR
stᴰ MONK & JOHN CLARK) *Mortally*

...THE PURSUIT
OF HAPPINESS'

July 4, 1776. The members of the Continental Congress signed the Declaration of Independence, and the United States of America was born. Justice and freedom ring through every word of this great national document:

From THE DECLARATION OF INDEPENDENCE

When in the course of human events, it becomes necessary for one people to dissolve the political bands which have connected them with another, and to assume among the powers of the earth, the separate and equal station to which the Laws of Nature and of Nature's God entitle them, a decent respect to the opinions of mankind requires that they should declare the causes which impel them to the separation.

We hold these truths to be self-evident, that all men are created equal, that they are endowed by their Creator with certain unalienable rights, that among these are life, liberty and the pursuit of happiness. That to secure these rights, governments are instituted among men, deriving their just powers from the consent of the governed. That whenever any form of government becomes destructive of these ends, it is the right of the people to alter or to abolish it, and to institute new government, laying its foundation on such principles and organizing its powers in such form, as to them shall seem most likely to effect their safety and happiness. . . .

We, therefore, the Representatives of the United States of America, in General Congress assembled, appealing to the Supreme Judge of the world for the rectitude of our intentions, do, in the name, and by authority of the good people of these Colonies, solemnly publish and declare, That these United Colonies are, and of right ought to be Free and Independent States; that they are absolved from all allegiance to the British Crown, and that all political connection between them and the State of Great Britain, is and ought to be totally dissolved; and that as Free and Independent States, they have full power to levy war, conclude peace, contract alliances, establish commerce, and to do all other acts and things which Independent States may of right do. And for the support of this declaration, with a firm reliance on the protection of Divine Providence, we mutually pledge to each other our lives, our fortunes, and our sacred honor.

GENERAL WASHINGTON ACCEPTS

In June of 1775 George Washington stood before Congress and accepted the Appointment as Commander of the Revolutionary Army. Although he modestly expressed some concern about his abilities as a General, Washington proved later that he was more than equal to the task:

Mr. President: Tho' I am truly sensible of the high Honour done me in this Appointment, yet I feel great distress from a consciousness that my abilities and Military experience may not be equal to the extensive and important Trust: However as the Congress desires I will enter upon the momentous duty, and exert every power I Possess in their Service for the Support of the glorious Cause: I beg they will accept my most cordial thanks for this distinguished testimony of their Approbation.

But lest some unlucky event should happen unfavourable to my reputation, I beg it may be remembered by every Gentleman in the room, that I this day declare with the utmost sincerity, I do not think myself equal to the Command I am honoured with.

As to pay, Sir, I beg leave to Assure the Congress that as no pecuniary consideration could have tempted me to have accepted this Arduous employment, (at the expense of my domestic ease and happiness) I do not wish to make any profit from it: I will keep an exact Account of my expenses; those I doubt not they will discharge, and that is all I desire.

THE COLONIAL ARMY

Though their fighting ability was great, the Revolutionary troops did not cut as dashing a figure as the Redcoats. Here is an eloquent description of General Washington's men written by the Chevalier de Pontgibaud, a French Count serving as a volunteer with the American forces:

Soon I came in sight of the camp. My imagination had pictured an army with uniforms, the glitter of arms, standards, etc., in short, military pomp of all sorts. Instead of the imposing spectacle I expected, I saw, grouped together or standing alone, a few militiamen, poorly clad, and for the most part without shoes—many of them badly armed, but all well supplied with provisions, and I noticed that tea and sugar formed part of their rations. . . . In passing through the camp I also noticed soldiers wearing cotton nightcaps under their hats, and some having for cloaks or greatcoats coarse woolen blankets, exactly like those provided for the patients in our French hospitals. I learned afterwards that these were the officers and generals.

Such, in strict truth, was, at the time I came amongst them, the appearance of this armed mob, the leader of whom was the man who has rendered the name of Washington famous; such were the colonists—unskilled warriors who learned in a few years how to conquer the finest troops that England could send against them.

A LITTLE HERO

Children were no strangers to the war. They often surprised the British with commando-type tactics, as did a young boy in 1776 in the following account from a contemporary journal:

It happened in 1776, that the garden of a widow, which lay between the American and British camps in the neighborhood of New York, was frequently robbed at night. Her son, a mere boy, and small for his age, having obtained his mother's permission to find out and secure the thief, in case he should return, concealed himself with a gun among the weeds. A strapping highlander, belonging to the British grenadiers came, and having filled a large bag, threw it over his shoulder; the boy then left his covert, went softly behind him, cocked his gun, and called out to the fellow, "You are my prisoner: if you attempt to put your bag down, I will shoot you dead; go forward in that road." The boy kept close behind him, threatened, and was constantly prepared to execute his threats. Thus the boy drove him into the American camp, where he was secured. When the grenadier was at liberty to throw down his bag, and saw who had made him prisoner, he was extremely mortified, and exclaimed, "a British grenadier made prisoner by such a brat!" The American officers were highly entertained with the adventure, made a collection for the boy, and gave him several pounds. He returned, fully satisfied for the losses his mother sustained.

A SOLDIER'S WIFE

In 1777 the British waged a heavy campaign along the Hudson River, with the support of German troops commanded by Baron Riedesel. His wife describes conditions for women who accompanied their soldier-husbands, and the defeat at Saratoga:

When the army again moved, on the 11th of September, 1777, it was at first intended to leave me behind; but upon my urgent entreaties, and as other ladies were to follow the army, I received, finally, the same permission. We made only small day's marches, and were very often sick; yet always contented at being allowed to follow. I had still the satisfaction of daily seeing my husband. A great part of my baggage I had sent back, and had kept only a small summer wardrobe. In the beginning all went well. We cherished the sweet hope of a sure victory, and of coming into the "promised land"; and when we passed the Hudson river, and General Burgoyne said, "The English never lose ground," our spirits were greatly exhilarated.

I had a large calash made for me, in which I, my children, and both my women servants had seats;

and in this manner I followed the army, in the midst of the soldiers, who were merry, singing songs, and burning with a desire for victory. We passed through boundless forests and magnificent tracts of country, which, however, were abandoned by all the inhabitants, who fled before us, and re-enforced the army of the American general, Gates.

On the 7th of October, my husband, with the whole general staff, decamped. Our misfortunes may be said to date from this moment. I had just sat down with my husband at his quarters to break-fast. General Frazer, and, I believe, Generals Bur-goyne and Phillips, also were to have dined with me on that same day. I observed considerable movement among the troops. My husband there-upon informed me, that there was to be a recon-naissance, which, however, did not surprise me, as this often happened. On my way homeward, I met many savages in their war-dress, armed with guns. To my question where they were going, they cried out to me, "War! war!" which meant that they were going to fight. This completely overwhelmed me, and I had scarcely got back to my quarters, when I heard skirmishing, and firing, which by de-grees, became constantly heavier, until, finally, the noises became frightful. It was a terrible cannon-ade, and I was more dead than alive.

Toward evening (Oct. 9th), we at last came to Saratoga, which was only half an hour's march from the place where we had spent the whole day. I was wet through and through by the frequent rains, and was obliged to remain in this condition the entire night, as I had no place whatever where I could change my linen. I, therefore, seated myself before a good fire, and undressed my children; after which, we laid ourselves down together upon some straw. I asked General Phillips, who came up to where we were, why we did not continue our retreat while there was yet time, as my husband had pledged himself to cover it, and bring the army through? "Poor woman," answered he, "I am amazed at you! completely wet through, have you still the courage to wish to go further in this weather! Would that you were only our commanding general! He halts because he is tired, and intends to spend the night here and give us a supper."

General Burgoyne was never able to resume the retreat. On October 17, he surrendered to General Gates:

At last, my husband sent to me a groom with a message that I should come to him with our children. I, therefore, again seated myself in my dear calash; and, in the passage through the American camp, I observed, with great satisfaction, that no one cast at us scornful glances. On the contrary, they all greeted me, even showing compassion on their countenances at seeing a mother with her little children in such a situation. I confess that I feared to come into the enemy's camp, as the thing was so entirely new to me. When I approached the tents, a noble looking man came toward me, took the children out of the wagon, embraced and kissed them, and then with tears in his eyes helped me also to alight. "You tremble," said he to me, "fear nothing." "No," replied I, "for you are so kind, and have been so tender toward my children, that it has inspired me with courage."

The Baroness Riedesel was not always exposed to the dangerous and tedious environment of battle. Here she describes a more pleasant interlude.

We made at Frederick Spring the acquaintance of Gen. Washington's family, and also of Madame Garel (a very lovable woman) and her husband. She was an ardent American patriot, but reasonable; and we became great friends. She spent most of the forenoons with us. At such times a Capt. Geismar played the violin, and I sang Italian airs, which gave her the greatest delight. One day, while thus engaged, a countryman, from whom we had endeavored by many kind words to obtain fresh butter, came in upon us. As the Americans generally are fond of music, he listened attentively, and, when I had finished, asked me to sing it once more. I asked him sportively what he would give me for it, as I did nothing gratis. "Two pounds of butter," he at once answered. The idea pleased me, and I began to sing. "Play another one," said he as soon as I had finished, "but something lively." At length I sang so much, that, the next morning, he brought me four or five pounds of fresh butter. He also had his wife with him, and entreated me to sing once more. I thus succeeded in winning their affection; and afterwards I lacked for nothing. The best of the joke was, that he actually believed I wished to be paid for my singing, and wondered much when I paid him for the butter, which he supposed they had already sold.

This tavern sign dates from about 1860 and depicts General Stark at the Battle of Bennington. Proprietor of the Inn was Eugene Noyes of Newbury, Massachusetts.

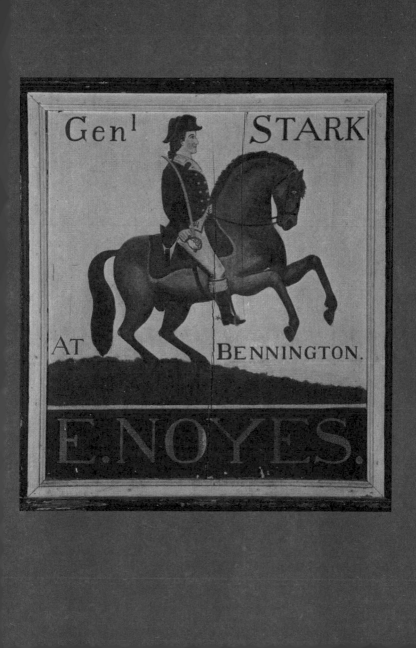

Genl STARK

AT   BENNINGTON.

E. NOYES.

THE STARS AND STRIPES

On June 14, 1777, at Philadelphia, Congress passed the following resolution:

Resolved, That the flag of the thirteen United States be thirteen stripes, alternate red and white. That the union be thirteen stars, white in a blue field, representing a new constellation.

The flag was officially first unfurled in battle in August of 1777 at Fort Stanwix, renamed Shulyer, in New York State. Soon thereafter the Stars and Stripes were raised on land and sea as the new symbol of America. An anonymous poem written at the time describes the new flag's inspiration:

> The red as of the rosy morn
> When brightest, clearest days are born,
> And of the lily fair and white
> When dipped in dews of summer night.
> The blue of clear and peaceful sky,
> When not a cloud goes floating by.
> The stars of brightest glittering
> All in that noble offering.
> This emblem, then, shall ever be
> The symbol of sweet liberty.

The flag was further described in the following words, ascribed to George Washington:

We take the stars from heaven, the red from our mother country, separating it by white stripes, thus showing that we have separated from her, and the white stripes shall go down to posterity, representing liberty.

MARTHA WASHINGTON

Part of Martha Washington's role in the long war, as she followed her husband wherever possible, may be seen in this description by a Mrs. Westlake, a resident of Valley Forge:

I never in my life knew a woman so busy from early morning until late at night as was Lady Washington, providing comforts for the sick soldiers. Every day, excepting Sunday, the wives of officers in camp, and sometimes other women, were invited to Mr. Potts'—Washington's Valley Forge headquarters—to assist her in knitting socks, patching garments, and making shirts for the poor soldiers, when materials could be procured. Every fair day she might be seen, with basket in hand, and with a single attendant, going among the huts, seeking the keenest and most needy sufferers, and giving all the comforts to them in her power. I sometimes went with her, for I was a stout girl, sixteen years old. On one occasion she went to the hut of a dying sergeant, whose young wife was with him. His case seemed to particularly touch the heart of the good lady, and after she had given him some wholesome food she had prepared with her own hands, she knelt down by his straw pallet and prayed earnestly for him and his wife with her sweet and solemn voice. I shall never forget the scene.

ROMANCE DURING THE REVOLUTION

*The comings and goings of dashing British sol-
diers, who often were quartered in private homes,
led to many romantic interludes with young Colonial lasses. Sometimes true love blossomed, and in
spite of the ill fortunes of war, eventually was ful-
filled. Two accounts follow, one from the diary of
an anonymous lady in Virginia, the other from a
collection of tales published shortly after the war
came to an end:*

My father was very hospitable and used to entertain all the strangers of any note that came among
us, and especially the captains and officers of the
British Navy that used to visit our waters before
the war. Among these I remember particularly
Capt. Gill, a fine old man, afterwards Admiral
Gill. He commanded at this time a fifty gun ship
called the Lanneston. . . . He had thirty-two mid-
shipmen on board, mostly boys and lads of good
families and several of them sprigs of nobility.

33

These used to come to my father's house at all hours and frequently dined with us. Sometimes, too, they would go into the kitchen to get a little something to stay their appetites, when old Quashabee would assert her authority, and threaten to pin a dish—something to their young lordships if they did not get out of the way. I remember particularly a young stripling by the name of Lord George Gordon, afterwards so famous as the leader of the riots in London, whom I have seen begging old Quashabee for a piece of the skin which she had just taken off the ham which she was about to send into the house for dinner, and eating it with great relish. Of course I had many beaux who flattered me and danced with me, and one or two who loved me, and would have married me if I would have said yes. Among these was a young Mr. Smith, a lieutenant in the British Navy with a fine florid face and auburn hair, who came here in a merchant vessel on his way to join his ship in the West Indies, who would have given his eyes for me if I would have taken them.

In this account, the daughter of a rebel proved a very strong attraction to English officers stationed near her father's inn. Love sprang up between the girl and a certain young adjutant by the name of Crookshanks, and they became engaged. The fu-

ture, however, looked unpromising, for the war seemed far from over:

One night the adjutant, and several of his comrades, slept under the rebel innkeeper's roof. It chanced to be the very occasion when Georgetown was surprised by the whigs. At early morn, the young lady was suddenly awakened by the reports of muskets, the clashing of swords, and the shouts of combatants, among which she recognized her lover's voice. In the greatest alarm, she sprang from her bed, and rushed, half dressed, out upon the piazza, where, to her terror, she saw her lover surrounded by a body of her countrymen, whose swords already hung suspended over his head, and threatening him with instant destruction. With a quick cry she sprang forward, rushed before the swords of his assailants, and threw herself upon his neck, exclaiming, "O save! save Major Crookshanks!" The sudden appearance of such a protector, coupled with admiration for her heroism, completely disarmed his opponents. He was taken prisoner, but released on his parole, and suffered to remain with his betrothed. The possession of so brave and true-hearted a woman, and the remembrance of this signal deliverance, no doubt, contributed in after years to the worthy adjutant's happiness.

YANKEE DOODLE

Every one is familiar with the traditional verse of this "children's" song:

> Yankee Doodle went to town
> A riding on a pony,
> He stuck a feather in his cap
> And call it macaroni!
>
> Yankee Doodle, keep it up,
> Yankee Doodle, dandy,
> Mind the music and the step,
> And with the girls be handy.

Its origin, however, is somewhat obscure. Most probably "Yankee Doodle" was written by a British Army surgeon sometime in 1775 to mock the raw Colonial troops. For some reason the tune later caught on with the Americans, who added their own words to it. Here are some of the verses recorded during the war:

> There was Captain Washington,
> Upon a slapping stallion,
> A-giving orders to his men—
> I guess there was a million.

And there they'd fife away like fun,
And play on cornstalk fiddles,
And some had ribbons red as blood,
All wound about their middles.

The troopers, too, would gallop up,
And fire right in our faces;
It scar'd me almost half to death,
To see them run such races.

LAFAYETTE IN AMERICA

*Largely due to the efforts of Benjamin Franklin,
France agreed to aid the American cause openly in
February, 1778. Among the best-known French
military leaders to serve in America were the
Count de Rochambeau and the young and dashing
Marquis de Lafayette. The following is from a
letter that Lafayette wrote to his wife upon arriv-
ing in America:*

Charleston, 19 June, 1777

I landed after having sailed several days along a
coast which swarmed with hostile vessels. When I
arrived, everybody said that my vessel must in-
evitably be taken, since two British frigates block-
aded the harbour. I even went so far as to send

orders to the captain, both by land and sea, to put the men on shore and set fire to the ship, if not yet too late. By a most wonderful good fortune, a gale obliged the frigates to stand out to sea for a short time. My vessel came in at noon-day, without meeting friend or foe.

I will now tell you about the country and its inhabitants. They are as agreeable as my enthusiasm had painted them. Simplicity of manners, kindness, love of country and of liberty, and a delightful equality every where prevail. The wealthiest man and the poorest are on a level; and, although there are some large fortunes, I challenge anyone to discover the slightest difference between the manners of these two classes respectively towards each other. I first saw the country life at the house of Major Huger. I am now in the city, where everything is very much after the English fashion, except that there is more simplicity, equality, cordiality, and courtesy here than in England. The city of Charleston is one of the handsomest and best built, and its inhabitants among the most agreeable, that I have ever seen. The American women are very pretty, simple in their manners, and exhibit a neatness, which is everywhere cultivated even more studiously than in England. What most charms me is, that all the citizens are brethren. In America, there are no poor, nor even what we call peasantry. Each individual has his own honest property, and the same rights as the most wealthy landed proprietor. The inns are very different from those of Europe; the host and hostess sit at table with you, and do the honors of a comfortable meal; and, on going away, you pay your bill without higgling. When one does not wish to go to an inn, there are country-houses where the title of a good American is a sufficient passport to all those civilities paid in Europe to one's friend.

I must leave off for want of paper and time; and if I do not repeat to you ten thousand times that I love you, it is not from any want of feeling, but from modesty; since I have the presumption to hope that I have already convinced you of it. The night is far advanced, and the heat dreadful. I am devoured by insects; so, you see, the best countries have their disadvantages. Adieu.

Overleaf: The Battle of Princeton, by William Mercer. Painted by the deaf-mute son of an American general killed in the battle, this scene vividly captures the fury of war. The Princeton encounter was won by the Americans when George Washington and his troops forced a British retreat.

BUNDLING

Certain customs of America caused the invading Englishmen some anxious moments, as evidenced by this letter written in 1777 by Lt. Thomas Anburey of the British Army:

The night before we came to this town (Williamstown, Mass.), being quartered at a small log hut, I was convinced in how innocent a view the Americans look upon that indelicate custom they call *bundling.* Though they have remarkable good feather beds, and are extremely neat and clean, still I preferred my hard mattress, as being accustomed to it; this evening, however, owing to the badness of the roads, and the weakness of my mare, my servant had not arrived with my baggage at the time for retiring to rest. There being only two beds in the house, I inquired which I was to sleep in, when the old woman replied, "Mr. Ensign," here I should observe to you, that the New England people are very inquisitive as to the rank you have in the army; "Mr. Ensign," says she, "our Jonathan and I will sleep in this, and our Jemima and you shall sleep in that." I was much astonished at such a proposal, and offered to sit up all night, when Jonathan immediately replied,

"Oh, la! Mr. Ensign, you won't be the first man our Jemima has bundled with, will it, Jemima?" when little Jemima, who, by the bye, was a very pretty, black-eyed girl, of about sixteen or seventeen, archly replied, "No, Father, not by many, but it will be with the first Britainer" (the name they give to Englishmen). In this dilemma what could I do? The smiling invitation of pretty Jemima— the eye, the lip, the—Lord ha' mercy, where am I going to?

Suppose how great the test of virtue must be, or how cold the American constitution, when this unaccountable custom is in hospitable repute, and perpetual practice.

TRAVELS WITH THE
MARQUIS DE CHASTELLUX

*The Marquis de Chastellux was a French noble-
man who travelled through North America during
the latter part of the war. He seemed to take little
interest in the conflict, but his observations during
the trip provide amusing and enlightening insights
about the life and times during the Revolution.*

*In his first narrative, the Marquis finds lodgings
for the night in the Connecticut farmhouse of a
Mr. Lewis:*

After dinner, about the close of the day, Mr. Lewis, who had been abroad on his affairs during a part
of the day, came into the parlour where I was,
seated himself by the fire, lighted his pipe, and
entered into conversation with me. I found him
an active and intelligent man, well acquainted with
public affairs, and with his own: he carried on a
trade of cattle, like all the farmers of Connecticut;
he was then employed in furnishing provisions for
the army, and was principally taken up in slaugh-
tering, and salting cattle for the state of Connecticut, to be sent to Fishkill. For each state is obliged
to furnish not only money, but other articles for
the army: those to the eastward supply it with cat-

tle, rum, and salt; and those to the westward with flour and forage.

At tea times Mrs. Lewis and her sister-in-law gave us their company. Mrs. Lewis had just recovered from lying-in, and had her child in her arms: she is near thirty, with a very agreeable face, and so amiable, and so polite a carriage, as to present a picture of decency itself, to every country in the world. The conversation was interestingly supported the whole evening. The family retired at nine o'clock; I did not see them in the morning, and paid my bill to the servants: it was neither dear nor cheap, but the just price of every thing, regulated without interest, and without compliments.

The Marquis describes a visit to some ladies in Philadelphia, among them a Mrs. Bache, the daughter of Benjamin Franklin:

That of the 22nd commenced like every other day in America, by a great breakfast. As the dinners are very late at the minister's, a few loins of veal, some legs of mutton, and other *trifles* of that kind are always introduced among the tea-cups, and are sure of meeting a hearty welcome.

After this slight repast, which only lasted an hour and a half, we went to visit the ladies, agreeable to the Philadelphia custom, where the morning is the most proper hour for paying visits. We began by Mrs. Bache; she merited all the anxiety we had to see her, for she is the daughter of Mr. Franklin. Simple in her manners, like her respectable father, she possesses his benevolence. She conducted us into a room filled with work, lately finished by the ladies of Philadelphia. This work consisted neither of embroidered tambour waistcoats, nor net work edging, nor of gold and silver brocade—it was a quantity of shirts for the soldiers of Pennsylvania. The ladies bought the linen from their own private purses, and took a pleasure in cutting them out, and sewing them themselves. On each shirt was the name of the married, or unmarried lady who made it, and they amounted to 2200.

JOHN PAUL JONES:
THE WAR AT SEA

The most famous naval battle of the war took place on September 23, 1779, off Flamborough Head, England, between the 50-gun British frigate Serapis *and the 40-gun American* Bon Homme Richard, *commanded by John Paul Jones. The battle raged for three hours, after which the* Serapis *struck her colors and surrendered. Lt. Richard Dale, deck officer of the* Bon Homme Richard, *recorded one of history's most memorable lines:*

I received orders from Commodore Jones to commence the action with a broadside, which indeed appeared to be simultaneous on board both ships. Our position being to windward of the *Serapis* we passed ahead of her, and the *Serapis* coming up on our larboard quarter, the action commenced abreast of each other. The *Serapis* soon passed ahead of the *Bon Homme Richard,* and when he thought he had gained a distance sufficient to go down athwart the fore foot to rake us, found he had not enough distance, and that the *Bon Homme Richard* would be aboard him, put his helm a-lee, which brought the two ships on a line, and the *Bon Homme Richard*, having head way, ran her bows into the stern of the *Serapis*.

We had remained in this situation but a few minutes when we were again hailed by the *Serapis*, "Has your ship struck?"

To which Captain Jones answered, "I have not yet begun to fight!"

FRANKLIN WRITES TO GEN. WASHINGTON

Benjamin Franklin spent much of the War on diplomatic missions abroad, successfully gathering aid for the Colonies. In the following letter to George Washington, the elder Statesman pauses at the mid-way point in the war to speculate on the future —his country's and his own:

Passy, March 5, 1780

Should peace arrive after another Campaign or two, and afford us a little Leisure, I should be happy to see your Excellency in Europe, and to accompany you, if my Age and Strength would permit, in visiting some of its ancient and most famous Kingdoms. You would, on this side of the

Sea, enjoy the great Reputation you have acquir'd, pure and free from those little Shades that the Jealousy and Envy of a Man's Countrymen and Contemporaries are ever endeavouring to cast over living Merit. Here you would know, and enjoy, what Posterity will say of Washington. For 1000 Leagues have nearly the same effect with 1000 Years. The feeble Voice of those grovelling Passions cannot extend so far either in Time or Distance. At present I enjoy that Pleasure for you, as I frequently hear the old Generals of this martial Country, (who study the Maps of America, and mark upon them all your Operations,) speak with sincere Approbation and great Applause of your conduct; and join in giving you the Character of one of the greatest Captains of the Age.

I must soon quit the Scene, but you may live to see our Country flourish, as it will amazingly and rapidly after the War is over. Like a Field of young Indian Corn, which long Fair weather and Sunshine had enfeebled and discolored, and which in that weak State, by a Thunder Gust, of violent Wind, Hail, and Rain, seem'd to be threaten'd with absolute Destruction; yet the Storm being past, it recovers fresh Verdure, shoots up with double Vigour, and delights the Eye, not of its Owner only, but of every observing Traveler.

The best Wishes that can be form'd for your

Health, Honour, and Happiness, ever attend you from your Excellency's most obedient and most humble servant.

B.F.

THE LADIES UNITE!

Citizens' (especially the women's) reaction to British occupation is illustrated by the following letter written by a British soldier from Charleston, South Carolina, in the spring of 1781:

I wish our ministry could send us a Hercules to conquer these obstinate Americans, whose aversion to the cause of Britain grows stronger every day.

If you go into company with any of them occasionally they are barely civil, and that is, as Jack Falstaff says, by compulsion. They are in general sullen, silent and thoughtful. The King's health they dare not refuse, but they drink it in such a manner as if they expected it would choke them.

The assemblies which the officers have opened, in hopes to give an air of gayety and cheerfulness to themselves and the inhabitants, are but dull and gloomy meetings; the men play at cards, indeed, to avoid talking, but the women are seldom or never to be persuaded to dance. Even in their dresses the females seem to bid us defiance; the gay toys which are imported here they despise; they wear their own homespun manufactures, and take care to have in their breasts knots, and even on their shoes something that resembles their flag of the thirteen stripes. An officer told Lord Cornwallis not long ago, that he believed if he had destroyed all the men in North America, we should have enough to do to conquer the women. I am heartily tired of this country, and wish myself at home.

Overleaf: Celebration of the Fourth of July, by J. L. Krimmel. After the signing of the Declaration of Independence on July 4, 1776, that date became a time of great annual celebration—a custom that has continued to our own day. This painting shows such a celebration in Philadelphia in 1819.

THE BRITISH SURRENDER AT YORKTOWN

On October 19, 1781, Lord Cornwallis surrendered his forces, numbering almost 8,000 men, to the combined American and French armies under Washington and Rochambeau. Cornwallis' defeat signaled the end of the British attempt to retain the colonies. A contemporary journal describes the scene of surrender:

At about twelve o'clock, the combined army was arranged and drawn up in two lines, extending more than a mile in length. The Americans were drawn up in a line on the right side of the road, and the French occupied the left. At the head of the former, the great American commander, mounted on his noble courser, took his station, attended by his aides. At the head of the latter was posted the excellent Count Rochambeau and his suite. . . . The Americans, though not all in uniform nor their dress so neat, yet exhibited an erect, soldierly air, and every countenance beamed with satisfaction and joy. The concourse of spectators from the country was prodigious, in point of numbers was probably equal to the military, but universal silence and order prevailed. It was about two o'clock when the captive army advanced through the line formed for their reception. Every eye was prepared to gaze on Lord Cornwallis, the object of peculiar interest and solicitude, but he disappointed our anxious expectations; pretending indisposition, he made General O'Hara his substitute as the leader of his army. This officer was followed by the conquered troops in a slow and solemn step, with shouldered arms, colors cased, and drums beating a British march.

GENERAL WASHINGTON RESIGNS

Appearing before Congress at the State House in Annapolis, Maryland, on December 23, 1783, George Washington delivered his address of resignation, from which excerpts follow:

Mr. President: The great events on which my resignation depended having at length taken place; I have now the honor of offering my sincere Congratulations to Congress and of presenting myself before them to surrender into their hands the trust committed to me, and to claim the indulgence of retiring from the service of my Country.

Happy in the confirmation of our Independence

and Sovereignty, and pleased with the opportunity afforded the United States of becoming a respectable Nation, I resign with satisfaction the Appointment I accepted with diffidence. A diffidence in my abilities to accomplish so arduous a task, which however was superseded by a confidence in the rectitude of our Cause, the support of the Supreme Power of the Union, and the patronage of Heaven. . . .

Having now finished the work assigned to me, I retire from the great theatre of Action; and bidding an Affectionate farewell to this August body under whose orders I have so long acted, I here offer my Commission, and take my leave of all the employments of public life.

WHAT IS AN AMERICAN?

*The following selection is taken from a book pub-
lished in 1782,* Letters From an American Farmer.
*The author, Jean de Crevecoeur, was in reality a
French nobleman—a pacifist and humanitarian
who wrote about agriculture in the colonies.*

*He lived in America for many years prior to the
Revolution, left during the war, and returned in
1783 as French Consul in New York:*

He is an American, who, leaving behind him all
his ancient prejudices and manners, receives new
ones from the new mode of life he has embraced,
the new government he obeys, and the new rank he
holds. He becomes an American by being received
in the broad lap of our great *Alma Mater*. Here
individuals of all nations are melted into a new
race of men, whose labours and posterity will one
day cause great changes in the world. Americans
are the western pilgrims, who are carrying along
with them that great mass of arts, sciences, vigour,
and industry which began long since in the east;
they will finish the great circle. The Americans
were once scattered all over Europe; here they
are incorporated into one of the finest systems of
population which has ever appeared, and which

will hereafter become distinct by the power of the different climates they inhabit. The American ought therefore to love this country much better than that wherein either he or his forefathers were born. Here the rewards of his industry follow with equal steps the progress of his labour; his labour is founded on the basis of nature, *self-interest;* can it want a stronger allurement? Wives and children, who before in vain demanded of him a morsel of bread, now, fat and frolicsome, gladly help their father to clear those fields whence exuberant crops are to arise to feed and to clothe them all; without any part being claimed, either by a despotic prince, a rich abbot, or a mighty lord. Here religion demands but little of him; a small voluntary salary to the minister, and gratitude to God; can he refuse these? The American is a new man, who acts upon new principles; he must therefore entertain new ideas, and form new opinions. From involuntary idleness, servile dependence, penury, and useless labour, he has passed to toils of a very different nature, rewarded by ample subsistence.— This is an American.

CHRONOLOGY 1775-1783

1775 April 19, Battle of Lexington and Concord.
June 17, Battle of Bunker Hill.
July 3, George Washington assumes
command.

1776 Jan. 20, British launch Southern Campaign.
May 2, France aids America with supplies.
June 28, Americans defend Charleston.
July 4, Declaration of Independence.
Aug. 17, Hessian mercenaries join British.
Nov. 16, Howe captures Ft. Washington.
Dec. 25-26, Washington crosses Delaware
River and defeats Hessians at Trenton.

1777 Spring, British raiding through New York,
Connecticut.
Aug. 16, Hessians beaten at Bennington.
Sept. 11, Battle of Brandywine Creek;
Howe out-maneuvers Washington.
Sept. 19, Battle of Freeman's Farm;
Burgoyne loses 600 men.

Oct. 17, Burgoyne surrenders to Gates.
Dec., Washington at Valley Forge.

1778 Feb. 6, France agrees to send troops
to aid Americans.
May 8, Howe is replaced by Clinton
as British Commander-in-chief.
July, Washington's march to New York;
first French troops arrive.

1779 May 8, Spain enters the War against Britain.
June-Sept., Successful campaign to remove
pro-British Indians from N.Y. and Pa.
Fall, American-British standoff.

1780 May 12, Charleston falls to Clinton.
July 11, Rochambeau, 6,000 French troops
arrive to join Americans.
Sept. 25, Benedict Arnold's Treason
discovered; he escapes to British.
Dec. 2, Gen. Greene commands Americans
in South, revives forces.

1781 Winter, American Troops mutiny in
Pennsylvania, New Jersey lines.
Spring, Greene follows Cornwallis;
battle of Guilford Courthouse is a draw.
May-July, Cornwallis' Virginia campaign;

he entrenches at Yorktown Aug. 1.
Sept. 8, Battle of Eutaw Springs.
Sept. 28, Americans-French march
on Yorktown.
Oct. 19, Cornwallis surrenders.

1782 Fighting diminishes; Nov. 14 is
probably last battle, in N. Carolina.

1783 April 15, Americans ratify Articles of Peace.
Sept. 3, Peace treaty signed in Paris.
Dec. 4, Last British Troops leave N.Y.
Dec. 23, Washington resigns.

Set in Caslon Old Style, a roman based on the designs
of the 18th century English typefounder William Caslon.
Printed on Hallmark Eggshell Book paper.
Designed by Rosalyn Schanzer.